BLUE SCREEN APOCALYPSE

The Impact of IT Failures on Modern Society

Cedric Yumba K

CONTENTS

INTRODUCTION

In our contemporary society, computer systems have become the central pillar around which a multitude of human activities are organized. They drive communications, manage financial transactions, control essential infrastructure, and facilitate work and entertainment. However, this technological interdependence has also led to unprecedented vulnerability. When a computer system fails, the repercussions can be colossal, affecting millions of people and causing significant disruptions on a global scale.

This book, "Blue Screen Apocalypse: Impact of Computer Failures on Modern Society," aims to closely examine these moments of failure, these instances where our systems falter, and society feels the tremors. Memorable incidents, such as the WannaCry viral attack in 2017 and the catastrophic Amazon Web Services outage the same year, illustrate how a single breach in the technological armor can sow chaos.

Through detailed case studies, we will explore not only the characteristics and causes of these failures but also their socio-economic impacts and the crucial lessons to be learned. We will delve into how these incidents have affected businesses, public services, and individuals, while also providing insights into prevention and adaptation strategies to avoid such scenarios in the future.

The objective of this book is twofold. On the one hand, it aims to raise awareness among a broad audience about the inherent risks of the technological infrastructure on which our modern world depends. On the other hand, it seeks to provide practical knowledge on best practices and innovations that can strengthen the resilience of these systems against inevitable failures.

Together, we will dissect these computer failures to understand their mechanisms, consequences, and corrective measures, in the hope of building a future where the "Blue Screen" is no longer synonymous with apocalypse but rather a manageable hiccup.

CHAPTER 1: INTRODUCTION TO COMPUTER FAILURES

The rise of technology in our daily lives has revolutionized the way we live, work, and communicate. However, this growing dependence on computer systems also exposes our society to significant risks in the event of failures. This first chapter lays the foundation for our exploration of computer failures, highlighting their potentially devastating impact and the need for robust strategies to prevent and manage them.

1.1 The Importance of Computer Systems in the Modern World

The digital age has profoundly and irreversibly transformed our daily lives. Computer systems are now embedded in the very foundations of modern civilization, acting as catalysts for innovation, efficiency, and global connectivity. Their importance manifests in almost every aspect of contemporary life, from commercial transactions to personal communication, to the management of critical infrastructure.

Take, for example, the healthcare sector. Computer systems are essential for the storage and management of electronic medical records, thereby improving access and accuracy of critical medical information. Technologies such as telemedicine and connected medical devices also enable remote healthcare delivery, reducing geographical barriers for patients. Moreover, large-scale data analysis helps predict epidemics and personalize treatments, thereby increasing the effectiveness of medical interventions.

In the financial domain, computer systems streamline transactions and banking operations. Global stock exchanges rely on sophisticated algorithms to process thousands of transactions per second, ensuring the smooth and efficient functioning of markets. Online banking services offer unprecedented convenience, allowing users to manage their finances from any location. This financial infrastructure relies on a complex and interconnected network of databases, servers, and security protocols.

Critical infrastructures, such as power grids and transportation systems, also heavily depend on computer systems. Smart power grids use sensors and software to optimize energy distribution, prevent outages, and integrate renewable energy sources. Air traffic and railway management systems rely on real-time calculations to coordinate schedules and ensure travel safety. Even water supply and waste management systems benefit from technological advances to improve their efficiency and resilience.

Modern businesses use computer systems to boost their productivity and competitiveness. Supply chain management software, for example, allows precise coordination of logistical operations, reducing delays and costs. Communication and collaboration platforms facilitate remote work and global collaboration, which has become more indispensable than ever during crises like the COVID-19 pandemic. The rise of e-commerce also relies on robust computer infrastructures that manage transactions, inventories, and deliveries, transforming consumer habits.

Personal communication and social networks are another area where computer systems play a central role. They allow individuals to stay connected with loved ones, share information instantly, and create virtual communities around common interests. Social media platforms, such as Facebook, Twitter, and Instagram, not only influence how we communicate but also how information spreads globally.

Education and research have also been revolutionized by computing. Online learning platforms and educational resources accessible via the internet have democratized access to knowledge, offering unprecedented learning opportunities. Computer simulation and modeling tools allow researchers to conduct complex experiments, process vast datasets, and develop new technologies faster than ever before.

The importance of computer systems cannot be overstated. They drive our economic, social, and technological progress, linking the various components of our modern society in a network of complex interdependencies. But this increased reliance comes with its own challenges and risks. A clear understanding of these systems and their importance better prepares us to face the inevitable disruptions they can cause.

1.2 Technical Failures

Technical failures represent one of the main causes of computer system failures. These failures can result from various sources, including software errors, hardware failures, and network interruptions. Each type of technical failure presents unique challenges and can have varying consequences depending on the context in which the failure occurs.

Software errors are common and can range from simple bugs to critical code defects. A notable example is the Google Maps application outage in 2016, which left millions of users without access to navigation services for several hours. A small error in the code can quickly propagate and affect interconnected systems unpredictably, leading to large-scale malfunctions. During the 2017 AWS incident, a single incorrect command during routine maintenance caused the unavailability of many online services for hours, causing considerable disruptions for several businesses.

Hardware failures are another major source of technical failures. The physical components of computer systems, such as servers, hard drives, and routers, are subject to wear and can unexpectedly fail. A notable example of hardware failure is the massive Microsoft Azure outage in 2013, caused by a failure in the cooling systems in a data center, resulting in server overheating and service shutdowns for thousands of users. Similarly, a hardware failure in a British Airways data center in 2017 led to the cancellation of hundreds of flights and major disruptions in airline services, affecting thousands of passengers.

Network interruptions represent another category of technical failures often difficult to predict and manage. Computer networks connecting different entities worldwide are vulnerable to various types of disruptions, including submarine cable cuts, router configuration issues, and network congestion. For example, in 2008, several submarine cables connecting Europe to Asia were simultaneously damaged, causing massive internet communication disruptions throughout the region. Network failures can paralyze communication systems, making online services inaccessible and disrupting business operations.

Technical failures can also be exacerbated by the phenomenon of "cascading," where a failure in one system leads to successive failures in other interconnected systems. This was illustrated by the power distribution infrastructure failure in India in 2012, which affected more than 620 million people. A simple technical failure in the electrical infrastructure led to a cascade of failures in several regions, depriving millions of electricity for several hours and affecting essential services.

Managing and preventing technical failures require robust strategies and constant vigilance. Redundancy and diversity of communication paths are crucial to ensuring network resilience. For example, using backup networks and failover systems can minimize the impact of failures by allowing quick recovery of operations. Moreover, proactive maintenance practices and regular system testing can identify and correct vulnerabilities before they cause major failures.

Technical failures are inevitable in a world where technology dominates the fundamental aspects of our daily lives. The frequency and consequences of these failures underscore the need for resilient infrastructure and well-designed risk management strategies. A thorough understanding of the different types of technical failures and their causes is essential for anticipating and mitigating their impacts, ensuring optimal continuity of crucial services for our modern society.

1.3 Human Errors

Human errors represent another major source of computer failures, often more insidious because they result not from technical malfunction but from an action or omission by a person. These errors can take various forms, ranging from misconfiguration of systems to execution of incorrect commands, and from negligence in updates to ignorance of security protocols. Their impact is sometimes as dramatic as that of technical failures, but they are often harder to predict and prevent.

A classic example of a human error causing a massive failure is the Knight Capital incident in 2012. This algorithmic trading company lost about $440 million in just 45 minutes due to a defective software update. A simple configuration error during deployment caused a chain reaction of erroneous trades, illustrating how a human error in a highly computerized environment can have disastrous consequences in a very short time.

Human errors can also occur during regular maintenance procedures. For example, in 2017, a human error caused a major outage of Uber's service in Europe. Engineers were performing a planned update when an incorrect command was executed, resulting in server shutdowns and service interruptions for millions of users for several hours. This type of error is particularly perilous because it often occurs during routine tasks, where a sense of complacency can set in.

Human errors are not limited to misguided actions; they also include omissions. A relevant example is the Delta Airlines incident in 2016. A series of computer failures was triggered by the omission to follow standard procedures for rebooting computer systems after a power outage. This negligence rendered the systems unavailable for long hours, affecting thousands of flights and hundreds of thousands of passengers.

Another crucial aspect of human errors is ignorance or noncompliance with security protocols. The famous Target attack in 2013, one of the largest data breaches in history, was facilitated by employees' lack of vigilance regarding computer security. Hackers accessed Target's systems via a third-party vendor, exploiting a negligence in applying security measures. This led to the theft of millions of customers' credit card information. This incident shows how poorly informed or lax human behaviors can create exploitable breaches in cybersecurity.

Inadequate employee training on new technologies and operational systems is another source of human errors. When a new system or procedure is introduced without adequate training, the risk of errors increases significantly. For example, the migration to a new patient management software in a Midwestern American hospital led to a series of programming and data entry errors because the staff had not been sufficiently trained in using the new system. These errors had direct consequences on the quality of care provided, illustrating the danger of underestimating the importance of staff training.

Human errors are also exacerbated by stressful or poorly managed work environments. Work overload, tight deadlines, and fatigue can make employees more prone to making mistakes. The crash of the Robinhood application in 2020, which left millions of users unable to buy or sell stocks during a period of market volatility, is partly attributed to high-pressure working conditions. Overworked engineers made hasty decisions and neglected some crucial verification procedures.

To mitigate the risks associated with human errors, it is essential to establish rigorous procedures, promote a culture of vigilance and responsibility, and ensure adequate and continuous employee training. Companies must also establish strong quality controls, regular audits, and well-established disaster recovery plans. Thus, although human errors are inevitable, their repercussions can be minimized through effective mitigation strategies. These measures will protect critical systems from preventable failures and maintain operational resilience in the face of human error.

1.4 Malicious Acts

Malicious acts, perpetrated by cybercriminals, hacktivists, or state actors, represent another major source of computer failures. These attacks are often designed to cause damage, steal sensitive data, or disrupt operations. Motivations can range from financial gain to political or ideological intentions, making these threats all the more complex and dangerous.

One of the most famous and devastating malicious attacks in recent history is the WannaCry ransomware attack, which ravaged computer systems worldwide in May 2017. WannaCry exploited a vulnerability in Windows systems, encrypting users' files and demanding a ransom to restore access. The UK's National Health Service (NHS) was particularly hard hit, causing the cancellation of thousands of medical appointments and delays in patient care. The economic and social consequences were enormous, revealing how a single malicious act can paralyze essential services.

Another striking example is the distributed denial-of-service (DDoS) attack on Dyn, an internet domain management company, in October 2016. This attack used a massive network of infected devices, such as surveillance cameras and home routers, to flood Dyn's servers with traffic, making them inaccessible. As a result, many major websites, including Twitter, Netflix, and Reddit, experienced significant service interruptions. This attack showed how seemingly innocent and mundane devices could be turned into powerful weapons by malicious attackers.

Cyberattacks motivated by geopolitical intentions are a growing threat. The hacking of American software company SolarWinds, discovered in December 2020, is a relevant example. Attackers suspected of working for a nation-state compromised SolarWinds' supply chain by adding malicious code to its software updates. This malware infected about 18,000 SolarWinds customers, including US government agencies, tech companies, and critical infrastructure, allowing attackers to spy and exfiltrate sensitive data for months before being detected.

Attacks targeting critical infrastructure are particularly concerning. In December 2015, a sophisticated cyberattack targeted the Ukrainian power grid, cutting off electricity to hundreds of thousands of homes for several hours. Attackers used malware to take control of power distribution systems, deliberately interrupting services. This incident demonstrates how malicious actors can target vital infrastructure to destabilize entire regions.

Insider threats represent another dimension of malicious acts. Employees or contractors with privileged access to systems may, for various reasons, choose to commit malicious acts. The example of Edward Snowden, a former NSA employee who leaked classified documents, highlights the risks posed by insiders. Although his motivations were ethical and political, his actions exposed vulnerabilities and sensitive operations, compromising national and international security.

Attacks aimed at stealing or compromising sensitive data are also frequent. The Equifax hack in 2017, where cybercriminals accessed the personal information of over 147 million individuals, illustrates this type of threat. The stolen data included social security numbers, addresses, and financial information, creating a significant risk of fraud and identity theft for the victims. This breach highlighted the need for companies to rigorously protect their customers' sensitive data.

Finally, phishing and social engineering attacks continue to be effective methods for penetrating computer systems. Attackers exploit individuals' trust and gullibility to obtain their login information or install malware. A famous phishing campaign in 2016 targeted members of the US Democratic National Committee, compromising emails and internal information. These attacks exploit human vulnerability to open a breach in technical defenses.

Malicious acts, whether motivated by financial, political, or ideological reasons, can cause enormous damage to computer systems and society in general. The sophistication and determination of cyber attackers require robust defenses and constant vigilance. A better understanding of the various forms of cyber threats and appropriate protective measures can help reduce risks and strengthen system resilience in the face of these dangers.

CHAPTER 2: CASE STUDY: THE WANNACRY ATTACK

After laying the foundation of the threat posed by computer failures, we will now dive into one of the most notable incidents in recent years: the WannaCry attack. This case study will concretely illustrate how a security flaw can transform into a global crisis, affecting critical infrastructure and disrupting essential services.

2.1 Timeline and Description of the Incident

On May 12, 2017, an unprecedented wave of cyberattacks began to spread globally in the form of ransomware called WannaCry. This attack was made possible by exploiting a vulnerability in Microsoft Windows operating systems known as EternalBlue. This vulnerability had been discovered but not disclosed by the National Security Agency (NSA) in the United States and was made public by a hacker group known as Shadow Brokers in April 2017.

The first phase of the attack occurred over one day. It was characterized by the rapid and widespread dissemination of the ransomware, affecting organizations and individuals in more than 150 countries within a few hours. The attack typically started with the infection of a computer through malicious software download or by directly exploiting the system's vulnerability.

Once a computer was infected, the WannaCry malware encrypted the user's files, rendering the entire system unusable. A message then appeared on the screen, demanding a ransom in bitcoins to unlock the files. The initial amount demanded was $300 in bitcoins, but it increased if the ransom was not paid within a given timeframe. The message also threatened to destroy the files if the ransom demand was not met after a certain period.

The attack targeted a multitude of sectors, but some of the most striking impacts were observed in the healthcare sector, particularly within the United Kingdom's National Health Service (NHS). The NHS suffered significant disruptions, with dozens of hospitals and clinics unable to access electronic medical records and provide essential care. Ambulance services were disrupted, medical appointments rescheduled, and surgeries canceled. This paralysis highlighted the critical dependence of modern healthcare systems on their IT infrastructure.

The spread of WannaCry was facilitated by the malware's ability to replicate itself by exploiting the EternalBlue vulnerability. This created a snowball effect, where each infected computer could contaminate other machines within the same network. Enterprise and public infrastructure networks, typically interconnected and often poorly segmented, allowed WannaCry to spread quickly and efficiently.

The response to the attack was swift but highlighted significant cybersecurity gaps. Shortly after the attack began, a British security researcher known as MalwareTech accidentally discovered a way to activate a "kill switch" that halted WannaCry's spread. By registering a domain name embedded in the malware's code, MalwareTech temporarily disabled the ransomware's ability to replicate. This action prevented millions of additional computers from being affected, although it did not help systems already infected.

In summary, May 12, 2017, will be remembered as the day WannaCry sowed chaos worldwide, exploiting a critical security flaw to infiltrate vulnerable networks. The speed and scale of its spread surprised many security experts and underscored the global challenges in protecting critical infrastructure against cyber threats.

2.2 Propagation Mechanisms

WannaCry's devastating effectiveness relied on several sophisticated propagation mechanisms that allowed the ransomware to spread rapidly across global computer systems. Understanding these mechanisms is essential to grasp the extent of the attack and the vulnerabilities exploited by cybercriminals.

The starting point for WannaCry's spread was the exploitation of the EternalBlue vulnerability in Windows operating systems. This particular vulnerability allowed attackers to execute malicious code remotely on unpatched machines, i.e., computers that had not installed the security update provided by Microsoft in March 2017. Unfortunately, a large number of systems had not applied this patch, leaving a vast attack surface accessible to cybercriminals.

WannaCry propagated using a worm method, which enabled it to replicate without human intervention. Once a computer was infected, the malware automatically scanned the local network for other vulnerable machines. It then used the same EternalBlue vulnerability to infiltrate these new targets and continue its expansion. This autonomous propagation mechanism is one reason why WannaCry managed to infect so many systems in such a short time.

In addition to the EternalBlue vulnerability, WannaCry also incorporated a component named DoublePulsar, a backdoor exploit also leaked by the Shadow Brokers. DoublePulsar allowed the installation of additional malicious components on infected systems and provided finer control over targeted machines, making the attack even harder to eradicate.

WannaCry further exploited network file shares by accessing unsecured shared resources. If a computer on a network had shared folders accessible without sufficient authentication, the ransomware could easily spread using these access paths. This method was particularly effective in enterprise environments and infrastructures where file sharing is common.

The speed and efficiency of WannaCry's spread were also reinforced by the lack of network segmentation in many organizations. Network segmentation involves dividing a network into distinct subnets to limit the spread of infections. In environments where this practice was not in place, the ransomware could move laterally across the network much more easily, affecting a greater number of systems in record time.

Another crucial propagation factor was social engineering and spear-phishing, though less central in WannaCry's case compared to other ransomware. Initial infection vectors often included malicious attachments in targeted phishing emails, which, when opened, downloaded and executed the malware on the victim's machine. While WannaCry primarily spread via EternalBlue, phishing tactics also contributed to the initial proliferation of the infection.

The massive impact of WannaCry highlights the importance of keeping systems up to date with the latest security patches. The public disclosure of the EternalBlue exploit by the Shadow Brokers gave cybercriminals a significant advantage, especially against unpatched systems. Many companies and institutions had not applied the necessary updates in time, allowing the worm to spread unimpeded.

Finally, the accidental kill switch discovered by MalwareTech played a paradoxical role. Even though this switch ultimately helped stop the spread, before its discovery and activation, WannaCry had uncontrollably infected global networks by exploiting these effective and formidable propagation mechanisms.

Understanding these propagation mechanisms is crucial for formulating effective strategies to prevent and respond to ransomware attacks. The combination of unpatched vulnerabilities, unsegmented systems, and unsecured file shares made WannaCry formidable and highlighted critical gaps in the cybersecurity practices of many organizations.

2.3 Global Impact

The WannaCry attack made history due to its scale and global repercussions. Within a few hours, the ransomware had infected hundreds of thousands of systems in more than 150 countries, highlighting the vulnerability of many organizations' IT infrastructures. WannaCry's impacts were felt on multiple levels, affecting various sectors and disrupting the daily lives of millions.

The healthcare sector was one of the hardest hit, particularly in the United Kingdom, where the National Health Service (NHS) experienced significant disruptions. Dozens of hospitals and clinics were forced to postpone appointments, cancel surgeries, and divert patients to other facilities due to the inability to access electronic medical records. The ransomware paralyzed administrative and medical systems, posing considerable risks to patients needing urgent care. This disruption underscored the critical dependence of healthcare institutions on IT systems and the need for increased resilience against cyberattacks.

The telecommunications sector was also heavily affected. Telefónica, one of Spain's largest telecommunications companies, saw part of its systems impacted by the ransomware, forcing employees to shut down their computers to limit the malware's spread. This measure led to temporary service disruptions for customers, demonstrating how such an incident can paralyze even large tech companies.

Manufacturing companies and industrial infrastructures also felt WannaCry's devastating effects. French car manufacturer Renault had to halt production in several of its plants to contain the infection, leading to significant financial losses and supply chain delays. Companies in various sectors, from logistics to aviation, reported similar disruptions, illustrating the ransomware's far-reaching impact.

Public administrations were not spared either. Several ministries and government organizations worldwide saw their operations disrupted, affecting services to citizens. For example, Indonesia's national police and government agencies in Russia were among the victims, hindering their ability to provide essential services.

The geographical reach of the WannaCry attack also highlighted the disparities in IT security across different regions. Emerging economies, often less equipped to deal with such threats due to a lack of resources and outdated infrastructure, were particularly vulnerable. Companies and institutions in China, India, and South America reported significant disruptions, revealing glaring gaps in global cybersecurity preparedness and resilience.

Financially, the costs incurred by WannaCry were enormous. Although ransom payments varied, with some analyses suggesting attackers collected several hundred thousand dollars in bitcoins, the overall economic losses related to business interruption, system repairs, and security reinforcements amounted to billions of dollars. Companies had to invest massively in security audits, software updates, and employee training to prevent future similar attacks.

The psychological impact on the public and businesses was also significant. WannaCry instilled fear and uncertainty, highlighting the ever-present threat of cyberattacks and the destructive potential of ransomware. Cybersecurity companies saw an increase in demand for their services, reflecting a heightened awareness of the importance of IT security. Governments also responded by strengthening their cybersecurity policies and promoting international cooperation initiatives to combat cybercrime.

In conclusion, the global impact of the WannaCry attack was vast and profound, affecting various industries, public administrations, and individual users worldwide. The attack's repercussions revealed structural vulnerabilities in IT systems and underscored the need for increased resilience against this modern form of threat. The scale of the disruptions caused by WannaCry marked a turning point in the awareness of cyber risks and in the approach to cybersecurity globally.

2.4 Response and Resolution

The response to the WannaCry attack, although rapid, highlighted the complex challenges posed by large-scale cyberattacks. As the extent of the incident became apparent, global coordination was undertaken to contain and resolve the crisis. Government agencies, private cybersecurity companies, and individual researchers collaborated to mitigate the ransomware's effects and prevent its further spread.

The key intervention occurred almost by accident when a young British cybersecurity researcher known as MalwareTech discovered a kill switch embedded in WannaCry's malicious code. This specific endpoint, when registered, prevented WannaCry from continuing to replicate. MalwareTech successfully registered the domain, blocking the ransomware's propagation on many networks and slowing its spread. This fortuitous discovery was a crucial moment in the initial response to the attack, preventing millions of additional infections.

Meanwhile, IT teams at affected companies and institutions frantically worked to isolate infected computers, apply necessary security patches, and restore systems from backups. Microsoft released emergency security updates, even for unsupported operating systems like Windows XP, to help patch the vulnerability exploited by WannaCry. These actions illustrated the urgency of the situation and the commitment of major tech companies to protect their users.

Containment measures also involved disabling computers connected to infected networks, quarantining compromised systems, and disseminating security directives to users. Organizations advised their employees not to open suspicious emails or attachments to prevent further infections through phishing vectors.

Simultaneously, governments worldwide intensified their efforts to coordinate the response to the attack. The United Kingdom's

National Health Service (NHS) worked closely with the National Cyber Security Centre (NCSC) to restore health services and ensure continuity of care. Cybersecurity agencies like the Department of Homeland Security (DHS) in the United States and the Cybersecurity and Infrastructure Security Agency (CISA) provided resources and guidance to businesses and critical infrastructure to bolster their resilience against ransomware.

One of the main challenges in resolving the WannaCry attack was decrypting compromised data. The malware used robust encryption, and assurances about file recovery after paying the ransom were slim. Many companies and users refused to meet the cybercriminals' demands, preferring to rebuild their systems from secure backups. In some cases, decryption tools were developed by cybersecurity researchers, although their effectiveness was limited and often specific to certain malware variants.

Lessons learned from responding to WannaCry also led to systematic improvements in managing cyber incidents. Organizations were encouraged to review and strengthen their backup policies, adopt multi-layered security strategies, and promote a cybersecurity culture by training their employees to identify and avoid potential threats.

In response to WannaCry, efforts were made to improve international collaboration in cybersecurity. Conferences and meetings between experts from various countries were organized to share information on emerging threats and best practices in protection. Governments began working more closely with the private sector to enhance defense capabilities and develop more resilient infrastructure.

Finally, regulators and legislative bodies became aware of the critical importance of IT security. Legislative initiatives were introduced to impose stricter cybersecurity standards and increase corporate responsibility in protecting sensitive data and systems. Public trust and economic stability depended on governments and businesses' ability to prevent and effectively respond to future cyber threats.

In summary, the response and resolution of the WannaCry attack were marked by a combination of fortuitous actions, rapid containment measures, and international collaborations. The crisis highlighted persistent vulnerabilities in global IT systems and served as a catalyst for reforms and reinforcements in cybersecurity.

2.5 Lessons Learned

The WannaCry attack left a trail of destruction but also acted as a powerful catalyst for reform and improvement in cybersecurity practices. The lessons learned from this event are numerous and span various aspects of IT system management, security practices, and international collaboration.

One of the most obvious lessons is the crucial importance of regular updates and security patches. WannaCry exploited a vulnerability for which a patch had already been released by Microsoft several months before the attack. However, many organizations had not applied this update, illustrating one of the main weak points in security infrastructures: procrastination or negligence in applying patches. This incident prompted many companies to review and strengthen their patch management procedures to ensure critical security updates are applied without delay.

The attack also highlighted the necessity of regular and reliable backups. Organizations with robust and recent backups of their data were able to recover more quickly and with less loss than those that did not. The practice of maintaining offline backup copies, inaccessible from the same networks as production systems, has become a priority. This ensures that even in case of compromise, essential data can be restored without paying a ransom.

Network segmentation strategies were reinforced following WannaCry. The attack showed how unsegmented networks allow malware to spread rapidly. By segmenting networks, organizations can contain infections and limit damage to specific subnets rather than risking spreading throughout the entire infrastructure.

Another crucial lesson was the importance of rapid and coordinated intervention in case of an incident. MalwareTech's discovery and activation of the kill switch were critical in limiting the infection's spread. This underscored the importance of cybersecurity research and collaboration between researchers, companies, and government authorities. Organizations like the National Cyber Security Centre (NCSC) in the UK and the European Union Agency for Cybersecurity (ENISA) intensified efforts to facilitate this cooperation and coordinate responses to cyber incidents.

Internationally, WannaCry illustrated the need for improved cooperation and information sharing. Cyber threats do not respect national borders, and an effective response requires global collaboration. Consequently, agreements and collaborative frameworks between countries have been established or strengthened to share threat information, response methods, and technical solutions more quickly.

Cybersecurity education and training have taken on increased importance. Incidents like WannaCry have pushed companies to invest more in training their employees to recognize and respond to potential threats. Regular awareness and training programs have become essential to strengthen the first line of defense against cyberattacks.

Finally, WannaCry prompted deeper reflection on vulnerability disclosure policies. The vulnerability exploited by WannaCry had been discovered by the NSA and kept secret until it was leaked by the Shadow Brokers hacker group. This raised ethical and practical questions about vulnerabilities known by intelligence agencies and their responsible disclosure to vendors to fix these flaws before they are maliciously exploited.

In conclusion, the WannaCry attack offered numerous lessons on the necessity of prompt security updates, rigorous backup practices, network segmentation, coordinated global responses, and the importance of cybersecurity education. By learning these lessons, organizations and governments can better prepare to prevent and respond to future cyber threats, ensuring greater resilience against incidents of this nature.

CHAPTER 3: CASE STUDY: THE 2017 AWS OUTAGE

The WannaCry attack showed us the consequences of a cyberattack, but outages can also result from human errors. The next chapter focuses on the 2017 AWS outage, an incident that demonstrates how a simple handling error can lead to large-scale disruptions in the world of cloud services.

3.1 Origin and Trigger of the Outage

On February 28, 2017, Amazon Web Services (AWS), one of the largest cloud service providers in the world, experienced a major outage that affected numerous websites and online services. The outage was triggered by a simple human error during regular maintenance activity in the S3 (Simple Storage Service) data storage service in the US-East-1 region, one of AWS's most important and widely used data centers.

The incident began when an AWS maintenance engineering team undertook a debugging operation to resolve a performance issue in the billing subsystem. To execute this task, the engineers used a command to remove a small number of servers from the S3 system. Unfortunately, due to a typo, the executed command was incorrect and accidentally removed a much larger number of servers than intended. This handling error led to the sudden shutdown of two critical subsystems.

The first affected subsystem was the index management capacity service, which is responsible for managing the location information of S3 objects. The second affected subsystem concerned the storage placement servers, which oversee the rebalancing and allocation of storage capacities. These subsystems are essential to the operation of the S3 service, and their inaccessibility caused a major disruption in operations.

Due to the close dependence between these subsystems, their simultaneous shutdown triggered a domino effect. Other system components began to slow down and fail as they could no longer access the essential location information needed to store and retrieve data. Since the S3 service is a fundamental pillar for many other AWS services, the effects of this outage quickly spread across the infrastructure, affecting services such as EC2 (Elastic Compute Cloud), RDS (Relational Database Service), and Lambda.

The interruption had significant consequences for a wide range of websites and applications dependent on AWS. Popular services like Trello, Quora, Slack, Business Insider, and many other major sites were affected. Users encountered page loading errors, prolonged wait times, and, in some cases, complete service interruptions.

A few minutes after the outage began, it became evident that the impact was more severe and widespread than the engineering team had anticipated. AWS support and engineering teams were immediately mobilized to diagnose the problem and initiate recovery procedures. However, the complexity of the systems and the scale of the interdependent failures made the restoration much more challenging than expected.

The recovery process involved gradually restarting the affected subsystems and reintegrating the disconnected servers into the overall infrastructure. As the index management and storage placement subsystems came back online, other AWS services began to stabilize. Full operational restoration took several hours, during which engineering teams worked tirelessly to ensure a return to normalcy while avoiding further interruptions.

The February 2017 AWS outage was a stark reminder of the potential vulnerabilities even in the most advanced and widely used cloud infrastructures. It highlighted the critical importance of careful and precise management of maintenance operations and underscored the need for robust verification and balance systems to prevent such human errors.

3.2 Immediate Consequences for Services

The February 28, 2017, Amazon Web Services (AWS) outage had immediate and widespread consequences for a wide range of services dependent on the S3 infrastructure in the US-East-1 region. Due to the dominant position of S3 as a data storage service, many other AWS services and, by extension, the applications and websites relying on them were severely affected.

Among the most affected AWS services were Elastic Compute Cloud (EC2), Relational Database Service (RDS), Lambda, and Simple Queue Service (SQS). The dependence of these services on S3's storage functionalities meant their performance and availability were directly compromised. EC2 instances, which constitute the "muscle" of many commercial applications, experienced significant functionality disruptions, causing numerous hosted applications to fail. RDS, used to manage critical databases, also faced significant slowdowns and downtimes, severely disrupting critical business database operations.

Web applications using image, video, and other static content storage services via S3 experienced immediate interruptions. Sites like Trello, a globally used project management platform, reported widespread outages, making their services inaccessible to users. Quora, a popular question-and-answer platform, was also unable to load pages, causing considerable frustration among its users.

One of the most visible aspects of the outage was the disruption of communication services. Slack, the widely used professional messaging tool, reported issues with loading files and images, affecting communication and collaboration among teams. Similarly, online journals like Business Insider and The Verge experienced interruptions, as they could not load critical resources stored on S3, hindering their ability to provide real-time news to their readers.

Startups and small businesses using AWS to host their services particularly felt the pressure of this outage. Many startups rely heavily on AWS for their low-cost, high-availability infrastructure. The S3 outage revealed that even paid backup and recovery services might be insufficient if an entire region experiences a severe outage. These interruptions caused a temporary loss of confidence among some AWS users regarding the reliability and robustness of their services.

Large enterprises relying on automated services and code-driven infrastructures were particularly vulnerable. For example, the S3 outage compromised continuous deployment pipelines for many DevOps teams, slowing development and production cycles. E-commerce companies reported interruptions in their payment and order management systems, directly affecting their revenue during the outage.

In summary, the AWS outage had immediate consequences on a wide range of services, from project management and communication applications to media platforms and e-commerce services. This major interruption highlighted how a failure in a critical segment of the cloud computing infrastructure could have cascading effects on the global digital ecosystem. Businesses using these services faced the crucial importance of resilience and redundancy in designing their IT architectures.

3.3 Economic and Commercial Repercussions

The February 2017 Amazon Web Services (AWS) outage had significant economic and commercial repercussions felt across various industries and sectors. Due to businesses' increasing reliance on cloud services for their daily operations, the interruption of the S3 storage service led to substantial financial losses and disrupted business activities for many organizations.

Economically, the interruptions caused by the S3 outage resulted in a loss of productivity for many businesses. Project management platforms like Trello were unusable, preventing thousands of teams from progressing in their daily tasks. E-commerce companies were particularly affected, as order processing systems and online payment services relying on AWS were interrupted. Sales losses during peak hours of the outage were substantial, representing significant revenue shortfalls for retailers.

Industries dependent on data analysis and information processing also faced considerable pressure. With database services like RDS unavailable, businesses could not access critical information needed for real-time decision-making. This loss of access delayed decision-making processes, causing disruptions in supply chains and operational losses.

Direct financial losses were amplified by the costs associated with crisis management. Businesses had to mobilize additional resources to resolve technical issues, restore services, and minimize negative impacts on customers. Internal IT teams and cybersecurity service providers were called upon to stabilize systems and ensure a quick return to normalcy. These emergency initiatives incurred unforeseen costs that strained companies' operational budgets.

The reputation and trust of customers were affected, especially for businesses offering critical services based on AWS. Dissatisfied end customers with the interruption of services expressed their frustration on social media and other public platforms, potentially tarnishing these companies' brand image. As customer loyalty is often directly tied to service reliability, some businesses had to invest more in retention strategies and transparent communication to restore trust.

For Amazon Web Services itself, the outage highlighted vulnerabilities in its infrastructure and management processes. Although AWS quickly issued public apologies and provided detailed explanations of the incident, the outage impacted the perceived reliability of its services. Amazon's stock experienced slight fluctuations in the days following the incident, reflecting investors' concerns about the resilience of its cloud infrastructure.

Competing companies like Microsoft Azure and Google Cloud Platform sought to capitalize on the situation by highlighting the reliability and robustness of their services. Some AWS client companies explored multi-cloud strategies to mitigate future risks, diversifying their cloud service providers to avoid excessive dependence on a single provider.

Ultimately, the 2017 outage served as a stark reminder of the economic and commercial risks inherent in dependence on cloud services. Companies were prompted to review and strengthen their business continuity strategies, invest in failure prevention technologies, and establish more robust disaster recovery plans.

In conclusion, the economic and commercial repercussions of the AWS outage were vast and varied, affecting sectors from e-commerce to data analysis to project management and financial services. This incident highlighted the crucial importance of resilience and redundancy in cloud architectures and pushed companies to rethink their strategies to mitigate risks associated with the interruption of essential technological services.

3.4 Recovery and Restoration Strategies

The recovery and restoration strategies implemented by Amazon Web Services (AWS) and its clients during the February 2017 S3 outage were crucial in minimizing prolonged disruptions and restoring services. The return-to-normal process involved a series of technical actions and logistical coordination to resolve issues quickly and efficiently.

As soon as the outage occurred, AWS engineering teams were mobilized to diagnose the source of the incident. Quickly identifying the incorrect command as the primary cause allowed for precisely targeting the affected subsystems. The first step in recovery was to gradually restart the critical servers that had been accidentally removed, ensuring no additional damage or further disruptions were caused.

Restoring the index management and storage placement systems was an essential priority. Engineers worked to restore the servers' ability to properly handle storage and data retrieval requests. This process involved meticulous checks and adjustments to ensure files were re-indexed and accessible without alteration. Close coordination between the various engineering teams was vital to synchronize these efforts and avoid conflicts or additional errors.

For AWS clients, recovery strategies varied depending on the nature of their services and infrastructure. Companies that had previously adopted solid backup and redundancy practices were able to restore operations more quickly. Regular backup systems, combined with staging and testing environments, allowed some organizations to recover without significant data loss. Companies using multi-region hosting structures could redirect their traffic to unaffected AWS regions, minimizing the impact on their end users.

AWS also provided transparent and continuous communication during the recovery period. Regular updates were posted on status dashboards and through customer support channels to keep clients informed of repair progress. This transparency helped alleviate customer anxiety and provided them with the necessary information to plan their own recovery actions.

Implementing internal communication strategies was another essential aspect of recovery. Companies had to inform their employees of the progress made and provide them with guidance on how to continue working despite interruptions. Clear and prompt communication allowed for better coordination of resolution efforts and helped maintain team engagement.

Once critical systems began to stabilize, companies conducted audits of their internal procedures to identify points of failure and improve future resilience. This involved post-mortem reviews to analyze what worked and what needed improvement. Lessons learned from these analyses were documented and integrated into disaster recovery and business continuity plans.

For example, several companies strengthened their backup practices by implementing off-site backup solutions and instant mirror copy systems. Others invested in microservices architectures that offer better isolation of components, reducing the potential impact of future outages. Network redundancy and the use of multiple cloud providers were also strategies adopted to diversify risks.

Finally, AWS itself took measures to prevent a recurrence of such an incident in the future. The company improved its command procedures by introducing additional safety checks to prevent the accidental execution of critical commands. Advanced alert systems and validation scripts were integrated to detect and prevent similar human errors. Updating training processes and incident response protocols was also undertaken to better prepare engineering teams to handle emergency situations.

In summary, the recovery and restoration strategies following the AWS outage relied on a combination of gradual restoration techniques, effective communication, and strengthened resilience practices. These actions not only allowed services to be restored as quickly as possible but also provided valuable lessons to prevent future outages, thereby reinforcing the robustness of IT infrastructures and cloud services.

3.5 Lessons Learned
from the Incident

The 2017 AWS outage incident provided numerous essential lessons for businesses, cloud service providers, and cybersecurity professionals. These lessons covered aspects ranging from maintenance operation management to designing resilient architectures and crisis preparedness.

One of the main lessons from this incident is the critical importance of precision and rigor in maintenance operations. The outage was triggered by a simple human error during a routine update, underscoring the need to thoroughly verify and test commands and scripts before execution. Amazon Web Services introduced additional safeguards to prevent such errors in the future, demonstrating the importance of integrating layers of validation and security into operational processes.

Another key point is the necessity of redundancy and resilience in infrastructure design. The S3 outage highlighted the vulnerability of systems concentrated in a single region or dependent on a single provider. Businesses learned to diversify their risks by adopting multi-cloud strategies and distributing their workloads across multiple geographic regions. This diversification helps reduce the impact of regional outages and ensures a more robust service continuity.

Moreover, the incident emphasized the importance of regular and secure backups. Companies with reliable backups were able to recover more quickly and minimize data loss. This scenario reminded organizations of the importance of automating backup processes and regularly verifying the integrity and accessibility of these backups. Maintaining offline backup copies became a priority to improve resilience against future interruptions.

Transparent and proactive communication during a crisis was another major lesson. AWS provided regular and detailed updates on the outage situation, helping alleviate concerns and inform customers of repair progress. Companies recognized the value of internal and external communication during a crisis, quickly informing employees, customers, and partners of ongoing actions and expected service restoration timelines.

Planning and crisis simulation exercises also emerged as essential practices. Organizations realized the importance of preparing well-defined business continuity and disaster recovery plans and regularly testing these plans to ensure their effectiveness. Outage simulations, failover tests, and incident response exercises help identify weaknesses and improve team coordination and responsiveness in real situations.

Continuous training of technical teams was identified as a crucial element in strengthening operational resilience. The incident highlighted the need to regularly train engineers and system administrators on best practices for managing cloud infrastructures, security procedures, and error prevention measures. Companies invested in professional development programs to ensure their teams stay up-to-date with the latest technologies and security practices.

Finally, the need for increased collaboration among stakeholders was amplified by this incident. Companies saw the importance of working closely with their cloud service providers, cybersecurity experts, and regulatory bodies to better understand risks and develop common solutions. Information sharing, strategic partnerships, and industry forums were strengthened to promote a collective approach to IT resilience.

In conclusion, the 2017 AWS outage was a significant event that highlighted the vulnerabilities of modern cloud systems but also offered a wealth of valuable lessons. By improving operational rigor, diversifying risks, strengthening backups, enhancing crisis communication, planning and testing incident responses, continuously training staff, and fostering collaboration, organizations can build more resilient infrastructures and be better prepared to face future disruptions.

CHAPTER 4: OTHER NOTABLE INCIDENTS

W hile we have explored specific incidents in detail, it is crucial to recognize that computer failures are not isolated events. This chapter presents other notable incidents, offering an overview of various types of outages that have affected critical services and highlighting the need for constant vigilance in maintaining system resilience.

4.1 Google Cloud Outages

Google Cloud, one of the world's leading cloud service providers, has not been immune to outages despite massive investments in the reliability and resilience of its infrastructure. One of the most significant outages in Google Cloud's recent history occurred on June 2, 2019, impacting a large number of services and users across multiple regions. This outage highlighted specific vulnerabilities and provided important lessons for the future management of cloud services.

On June 2, 2019, a major outage hit Google's cloud services, causing disruptions to widely used platforms such as YouTube, Gmail, Google Drive, and Google Cloud Platform (GCP) itself. The incident originated from a network configuration issue affecting router resources. The outage began when Google engineers undertook a planned network configuration change, a common operation in IT infrastructure management. However, an error in the configuration deployment led to unexpected saturation of network links in the US-East1 region, one of Google Cloud's most heavily used availability zones.

This saturation caused significant delays in network traffic, complicating access to services for end users. Automated network management systems, designed to maximize availability by dynamically balancing traffic, were unable to effectively respond to this sudden overload. Consequently, users across multiple regions began experiencing long loading times, connection errors, and total service interruptions.

The impact of the outage was massive and immediate. YouTube, one of the world's largest video-sharing platforms, became inaccessible to millions of users, disrupting both content consumers and content creators who rely on the platform for their livelihood. Gmail, used by billions for personal and professional communications, experienced delays and errors in sending and receiving emails, affecting productivity and business operations.

Companies using Google Cloud Platform to host their applications and services were also severely affected. Startups and large enterprises reported website outages, application interruptions, and disruptions in real-time operations. E-commerce systems, financial services, and mobile applications all experienced slowdowns and failures, leading to revenue losses and customer frustration.

Google Cloud's response to the outage was swift. Engineers worked tirelessly to understand the extent of the problem and implement solutions to restore normal service operations. One of the first steps was to correct the faulty network configuration that led to the link saturation. Technical teams also dynamically rerouted traffic to less congested links, allowing for the gradual recovery of affected services.

Throughout the outage, Google maintained transparent communication with its users, providing regular updates on the status and recovery efforts through its communication channels. This transparency helped mitigate some user frustration and maintain trust in Google's ability to manage incidents.

Following the outage, Google Cloud implemented several improvements to prevent similar future incidents. The company strengthened its network configuration testing and validation procedures, increased automated monitoring to detect anomalies more quickly, and improved dynamic traffic distribution mechanisms. Google also intensified training for engineers and network managers to minimize human errors.

The June 2019 incident highlighted specific vulnerabilities in network management and the critical importance of redundancy and resilience in cloud infrastructure. Although Google Cloud is recognized for its innovation and overall reliability, this outage served as a reminder that even tech giants are not immune to errors and failures. By leveraging these lessons, Google has been able to bolster its systems and better prepare its services for future challenges.

4.2 Facebook Outage in 2021

On October 4, 2021, Facebook, along with its affiliated apps Instagram and WhatsApp, suffered a major outage that lasted nearly six hours, marking one of the most significant service interruptions in recent social media history. This outage had global consequences, disrupting personal and professional communications and highlighting the challenges and vulnerabilities of complex technological infrastructures.

The cause of this outage was attributed to a configuration change on the backbone routers that coordinate network traffic between Facebook's data centers worldwide. This modification disrupted the connections between data centers, triggering a cascade of effects that rendered Facebook's five main services inaccessible to billions of users. Technically, the outage was caused by a misconfigured routing update that cut off all connections to Facebook's Domain Name System (DNS) servers, making it impossible to resolve IP addresses needed to access its services.

The outage not only affected end users but also paralyzed Facebook's internal tools, making it difficult for engineers to diagnose and quickly resolve the problem. Facebook employees faced issues accessing buildings and systems, adding a layer of complexity to crisis management. Internal communication systems, blocked by the outage, forced teams to use external means to coordinate their recovery efforts.

The global impact was enormous. Facebook and Instagram users were unable to log in, post updates, or communicate via the platforms. For WhatsApp, widely used as the primary communication tool in many countries, the interruption disrupted crucial conversations, affecting families, businesses, and emergency services. Millions of small businesses that rely on these platforms for their commercial activities and customer interaction reported revenue losses and significant operational disruptions.

Companies using Facebook for advertising and marketing were also affected. The interruption prevented brands from launching ad campaigns, monitoring ongoing ad performance, and interacting with their audiences. This was particularly problematic due to the timing with product launches, promotions, and planned marketing events.

Facebook's response to the incident involved intense efforts to restore services and provide transparent explanations to users and investors. Once the routing problem was identified, engineers worked tirelessly to correct the configuration and restore connections between data centers. Recovery steps involved system restarts, service integrity checks, and rigorous testing to ensure no other part of the infrastructure was compromised.

Facebook's external communications provided regular updates on the recovery status, though some information was initially limited due to the nature of the problem. Messages and technical explanations posted on the company's blog and through other channels helped clarify the cause of the outage and the steps taken to prevent similar incidents in the future.

In the post-mortem analysis, Facebook conducted a detailed review of the incident to learn lessons and strengthen system resilience. Corrective measures included improvements to configuration update protocols, more extensive testing before deployments, and enhanced backup and redundancy systems to ensure service continuity in case of a similar incident. Facebook also reviewed its crisis management protocols to ensure access to critical internal tools is not compromised in a widespread outage.

The 2021 Facebook outage highlighted the vulnerabilities of large technological infrastructures and the importance of rigorous network configuration management. It was a reminder that even tech giants are not immune to operational failures and that the impact of such incidents can be profound, affecting millions of users and businesses dependent on these services. For Facebook, it was an opportunity to improve its systems and reinforce user trust in its ability to provide stable and resilient services.

4.3 Microsoft Azure Incident

On September 4, 2018, Microsoft Azure, one of the world's largest cloud service providers, experienced a major outage that affected millions of users worldwide. This interruption highlighted the vulnerabilities of cloud infrastructure and underscored the importance of resilience and redundancy in managing such complex systems.

The incident began when a powerful storm caused a power outage at Microsoft's West US data center. The initial power cut triggered a chain of failures affecting several critical services. Despite the presence of backup generators, the intensity of the storm damaged cooling infrastructure, impacting server performance and availability.

Once power was restored, problems persisted due to malfunctions in Microsoft Azure's storage systems. With cooling systems not immediately restored, servers overheated, causing hardware failures and data loss for some customers. Engineering teams worked tirelessly to repair the damage and restore services, but the recovery process was complicated by the need to preserve data integrity and ensure systems were secure before bringing them back online.

The outage, which lasted nearly 24 hours, had widespread repercussions for users of many Azure services, including virtual machines (VM), blob storage, SQL Database, and other critical cloud services. Azure customers experienced interruptions in accessing their hosted applications and services, disrupting business operations and daily activities for many organizations.

Online services dependent on Azure were also affected. Popular applications used by both consumers and professionals recorded slowdowns and interruptions. Companies using Azure for their critical APIs and backend systems reported difficulties in providing consistent services to their end customers. These interruptions caused considerable frustration and financial losses for many organizations.

Microsoft's response to the crisis involved intensive coordination among its engineering, support, and communication teams. Microsoft engineers undertook corrective actions to restore damaged cooling and electrical infrastructure. Simultaneously, efforts were made to recover lost data and securely relaunch cloud services.

Microsoft maintained transparent communication with its customers throughout the outage. Regular updates were posted via the Azure status dashboard and company communication channels. Customers were informed of the repair progress, causes of the outage, and measures taken to prevent future similar incidents.

After resolving the incident, Microsoft conducted a detailed post-mortem analysis to identify infrastructure and operational process improvements. This analysis highlighted the importance of failure prevention systems and the need to strengthen maintenance operations and incident response protocols.

Microsoft took several steps to prevent a recurrence of such events. The company improved redundancy systems for power supplies and cooling infrastructure, ensuring multiple backup levels are available even under extreme weather conditions. Rigorous infrastructure testing procedures and failure simulations were integrated into regular operational processes to ensure systems can withstand various emergency scenarios.

Additionally, Microsoft enhanced its automated monitoring mechanisms to quickly detect and respond to anomalies before they cause significant interruptions. The company also intensified training programs for engineers and system administrators, familiarizing them with best practices for managing cloud infrastructure and preparing them to effectively handle crises.

In conclusion, the 2018 Microsoft Azure incident illustrated the complex challenges cloud service operators face and provided valuable lessons on the importance of infrastructure resilience and proactive failure prevention. In response to this event, Microsoft took significant measures to improve its systems and processes, thereby strengthening the reliability and robustness of its cloud services to better meet the needs of its global customers.

4.4 Cloudflare Infrastructure Failure

On July 2, 2019, Cloudflare, one of the world's largest providers of internet infrastructure services, experienced a major outage that affected numerous websites and online services for about half an hour. This failure highlighted the inherent risks of centralizing critical services and the complexity of modern infrastructures. The incident had significant repercussions for many businesses and users worldwide.

The cause of the outage was quickly identified after the incident. An erroneous configuration deployment in one of Cloudflare's Web Application Firewall (WAF) policies led to CPU saturation on servers, causing a massive service interruption. Essentially, a misconfigured rule triggered an exponential increase in CPU usage, overloading systems and making websites and services dependent on Cloudflare inaccessible.

The impact of this failure was immediate. Cloudflare, which protects and accelerates millions of websites, saw a large majority of its clients affected. Users trying to access websites protected by Cloudflare received error messages, rendering many online services unusable. E-commerce sites, social media applications, news sites, and community forums all suffered from this interruption.

Businesses of all sizes, from small startups to large enterprises, felt the effects of the outage. Online retailers reported sales losses during the interruption, and communication platforms were unable to transmit messages and notifications in real-time. End users encountered frustrations trying to access essential services for their daily activities, adding pressure on support and customer service teams of affected businesses.

Cloudflare's response to the incident was swift and transparent. The engineering team immediately began analyzing logs and identifying the problematic configuration. Once the cause was determined, they deployed a fix to the affected systems, which helped gradually restore services. Communication with customers was maintained throughout the crisis, with frequent updates providing details on the recovery status and steps taken to resolve the issue.

In parallel with immediate resolution efforts, Cloudflare conducted a thorough post-mortem analysis to understand the flaws in their WAF configuration and deployment processes. The report published by Cloudflare detailed not only the technical causes of the incident but also the corrective and preventive measures implemented to avoid similar outages in the future.

Cloudflare improved several aspects of its internal protocols in response to this incident. First, the company implemented additional controls to validate configurations before deployment in the production environment. These measures include more rigorous automated testing and manual reviews by validation engineers to detect and correct potential errors before they affect production systems.

Second, Cloudflare strengthened its monitoring and alerting capabilities. Anomaly detection systems for CPU load and other abnormal resource usage were integrated to quickly identify and respond to overload situations before they cause massive interruptions. This proactive monitoring allows engineering teams to intervene more quickly and prevent cascading effects of a configuration error.

Third, Cloudflare increased its internal training efforts, focusing on best practices for configuration and rule management. Retraining programs and ongoing training were implemented to ensure engineers stay well-informed about security protocols and new validation tools.

Finally, Cloudflare invested in improving overall resilience through increased redundancy implementations and network route diversification. This includes establishing backup and failover systems to ensure interruptions in one service segment do not disrupt the entire infrastructure.

In conclusion, the 2019 Cloudflare infrastructure failure highlighted the technical and operational challenges faced by modern internet service providers. Despite the scale and impact of the outage, Cloudflare's measures to correct identified flaws and strengthen service resilience demonstrate a long-term commitment to the reliability and security of their infrastructure.

4.5 Other Notable Incidents

In addition to the major outages previously mentioned, other notable incidents have marked the recent history of cloud services and technological infrastructures. These incidents, although varied in their causes and impacts, illustrate the diverse challenges faced by technology companies and the potentially devastating consequences of service interruptions.

Google Maps API Outage (2018)

On July 15, 2018, a Google Maps API outage caused disruptions for millions of websites and applications that depend on the service to provide maps, routes, and geolocation services. This interruption was caused by a configuration update that introduced an overload on the API servers, making user requests impossible to process correctly. Companies using the Google Maps API in their transportation, delivery, and location-based services platforms reported significant service interruptions, affecting not only business operations but also the user experience.

GitHub Outage (2018)

On February 28, 2018, GitHub, the world's largest code hosting platform, suffered an unprecedented distributed denial-of-service (DDoS) attack. The traffic peak reached 1.35 terabits per second, saturating GitHub's infrastructure and making the site inaccessible for several hours. This attack forced GitHub to activate emergency countermeasures, relying on its DDoS protection provider to absorb the malicious traffic and restore services. The incident highlighted the vulnerability of collaborative development platforms and the importance of robust DDoS protection solutions.

Slack Outage (2020)

On February 1, 2020, Slack, one of the leading professional messaging platforms, experienced a major outage lasting over three hours. The incident was caused by a database overload following a cascade of unoptimized requests, causing delays and errors for millions of users worldwide. Companies using Slack for internal communication and collaboration faced interruptions, affecting productivity and team coordination. Slack quickly deployed fixes to overcome the database overload and improve the resilience of its communication services.

Oracle Cloud Outage (2021)

On January 7, 2021, Oracle Cloud experienced a significant outage that affected the services of several international clients. The incident stemmed from a software update that had not been properly tested before deployment, leading to failures in the identity and access management system. Oracle Cloud users had difficulty authenticating and accessing their cloud services, disrupting business operations and managing critical data. Oracle implemented emergency corrective measures to restore services and strengthened its software update validation processes to prevent similar future outages.

Akamai Outage (2021)

On July 22, 2021, Akamai Technologies, an internet infrastructure services company, experienced a DNS services outage that caused interruptions for many websites and online services, including e-commerce companies, financial institutions, and government platforms. The incident, caused by a misconfigured software update, highlighted the critical dependence on DNS services for internet connectivity. Akamai quickly corrected the erroneous configuration and reinforced its configuration management procedures to prevent future incidents.

Salesforce Incident (2019)

On May 11, 2019, Salesforce, one of the leading CRM solution providers, was hit by a permission issue that disrupted user access to their environments. A poorly deployed software update revoked access permissions for tens of thousands of users, making their accounts inactive and preventing access to critical CRM data and tools. The incident lasted several hours as Salesforce restored permissions and ensured a return to normalcy for its clients. This event highlighted the importance of update testing and rigorous permission management in cloud-based systems.

In conclusion, these notable incidents illustrate the diversity of potential causes of outages in cloud computing systems and internet infrastructure, ranging from configuration errors to malicious attacks and hardware failures. Each incident provided points of reflection and opportunities to strengthen service resilience, improve testing and deployment procedures, and develop recovery strategies for inevitable interruptions in an increasingly connected world.

CHAPTER 5: SOCIETAL CONSEQUENCES OF IT FAILURES

T he previous incidents have shown us the immediate effects of IT failures, but what are the longer-term repercussions? This chapter delves deeply into the economic and social impacts of IT failures, exploring how they can affect not only businesses but also individuals and national economies.

5.1 Impact on Public Services

IT failures can have devastating consequences on public services, endangering not only the daily operations of these services but also the safety and well-being of citizens. Incidents in critical infrastructures, including healthcare systems, transportation networks, emergency services, and public administrations, reveal how heavily modern society depends on technology for smooth functioning.

Healthcare Systems

One of the most striking examples of the impact of IT failures on public services concerns healthcare systems. During the WannaCry attack in 2017, the United Kingdom's National Health Service (NHS) suffered major disruptions. Dozens of hospitals and clinics were unable to access electronic medical records, forcing doctors and nurses to revert to paper methods for diagnoses and treatments. Many surgeries had to be canceled, emergency services were redirected, and care was delayed. This interruption not only resulted in significant financial costs but also compromised the quality of care provided to patients.

Transportation Networks

Transportation networks, including rail systems, airports, and traffic management systems, are also particularly vulnerable to IT failures. For instance, in July 2017, British Airways' IT systems failed, leading to the cancellation of several hundred flights and disrupting travel for thousands of passengers. The failure was attributed to a power outage followed by poorly managed system recovery. Failures in traffic management systems, such as traffic lights and control systems, can lead to massive traffic jams and increase the risk of accidents.

Emergency Services

Emergency services, such as police, fire, and ambulance services, heavily depend on IT systems for call reception and dispatch, coordination of interventions, and access to critical information.

Any failure in these systems can have fatal consequences. For example, a 911 system outage in the United States in 2020 caused delays in emergency call responses, compromising the ability of first responders to provide timely and effective assistance.

Public Administration

Public administrations, including municipal services, courts, and social services agencies, are also vulnerable to IT failures. In 2018, a ransomware attack on the Baltimore City Hall's IT platform paralyzed municipal services for several weeks. Residents encountered difficulties in making tax payments, obtaining permits, and accessing other essential services. The disruption of municipal services also resulted in significant financial losses for the city and highlighted the security flaws in public IT systems.

Energy Networks

Energy networks, including power grids and gas pipelines, rely on sophisticated industrial control systems to manage distribution and consumption. A failure in these systems can cause widespread power outages and interruptions in the natural gas supply. For example, the cyberattack on Ukraine's power grid in 2015 caused blackouts affecting hundreds of thousands of homes. This incident illustrated the potential consequences of cyberattacks on critical infrastructure and the need to strengthen the resilience of industrial control systems.

In conclusion, IT failures in public services can have extensive repercussions, affecting the health, safety, and well-being of citizens. These incidents highlight the importance of enhancing the resilience of critical infrastructure and implementing business continuity plans to minimize the impacts of inevitable outages. Technology plays a central role in our modern society, and any failure in IT systems can have significant and far-reaching consequences.

5.2 Consequences for Businesses

IT failures can have extremely severe impacts on businesses, affecting their operations, reputation, and finances. Whether due to technical failure, human error, or malicious attack, businesses across all sectors are vulnerable to service interruptions that can significantly disrupt their activities.

Operational Disruptions

IT failures can paralyze a company's operations, making critical tasks impossible and hampering productivity. For example, during the AWS outage of 2017, many companies using Amazon's cloud services saw their online applications and systems become inaccessible. This led to service interruptions for e-commerce platforms, streaming services, and other key applications. E-commerce businesses were particularly affected, with websites unable to process orders, leading to disruptions in sales and inventory management.

Data and Time Loss

System failures can also lead to the loss of essential data. Incidents of unplanned outages or ransomware attacks can compromise the integrity of a company's data, necessitating complex and sometimes unattainable restoration of lost information. During the WannaCry incident, several companies in the manufacturing and financial services sectors reported the loss of critical data and had to mobilize considerable resources to restore their systems and recover their information. The time spent recovering data is not only costly but also slows down the company's normal operations.

Financial Impact

IT failures have direct and indirect financial implications. Immediate costs include mobilizing technical support teams to diagnose and resolve issues, while indirect costs can include lost revenue due to service unavailability, compensation demanded by affected customers, and productivity losses. For example, the

Microsoft Azure outage in 2018, caused by a storm and prolonged power outage, cost many companies millions of dollars in lost business opportunities and productivity.

Reputation Damage

A company's reputation can also suffer from IT failures, especially if they visibly and significantly affect customers. In the case of the 2021 Facebook outage, individual users and businesses using the platforms for their commercial activities publicly expressed their frustration on social media and other forums. The inability to connect and use services for several hours damaged user trust in the company's reliability. Companies may need to increase their communication and crisis management efforts to restore their brand image and regain customer trust after such interruptions.

Impact on Customer Relations

IT failures can affect the relationship between the company and its customers, particularly if the services provided are critical to customer operations. For example, during the Cloudflare outage in 2019, many client companies faced interruptions in their own service, leading to customer frustration and reduced satisfaction. Expectations regarding service availability and reliability are high, and companies must be able to respond quickly and effectively to avoid damaging long-term relationships with their customers.

Compliance and Regulation

In some sectors, IT failures can also lead to regulatory complications. Financial institutions, for example, must comply with strict regulations regarding data security and operational resilience. Failures can attract regulatory scrutiny, leading to thorough investigations, financial penalties, and stricter compliance requirements. Prolonged exposure to outages can also create a perception of unreliability and increased pressure from regulators to strengthen security measures and service continuity plans.

In summary, the consequences of IT failures for businesses are considerable and multifaceted. They extend beyond immediate disruptions to include long-term impacts on reputation, finances, and customer relations. Companies must invest in robust resilience and crisis management strategies to mitigate the effects of inevitable interruptions and protect their operations and brand image. Learning from past incidents, such as the AWS, Microsoft Azure, Cloudflare, and other outages, companies can strengthen their infrastructure and implement emergency plans capable of ensuring business continuity despite IT challenges.

5.3 Effects on Individuals

IT failures, while primarily affecting large infrastructures and businesses, also have direct and significant repercussions on individuals. Whether in their daily lives, social interactions, or professional activities, individuals can experience a wide range of disruptions and inconveniences due to interruptions in technological services.

Disruptions in Daily Life

IT failures can disrupt many aspects of individuals' daily lives. For instance, during the 2021 Facebook outage, millions of people worldwide were unable to access their Facebook, Instagram, and WhatsApp accounts. These social media platforms play a crucial role in personal communications, event organization, and connecting with friends and family. The unavailability of services disrupted conversations, photo sharing, information exchanges, and the coordination of social activities, creating widespread frustration.

Inability to Access Essential Services

IT failures can also prevent individuals from accessing essential services. For example, during the 2017 AWS outage, online services such as online banking systems, payment platforms, and delivery services were interrupted, making it difficult for consumers to conduct financial transactions, pay bills, or track orders. This inability to access essential services can cause major inconveniences, especially for those who heavily rely on online services for their daily needs.

Interruption of Professional Activities

For professionals, IT failures can lead to significant interruptions in their work activities. Remote workers, for example, often rely on online communication and collaboration platforms such as Slack or Microsoft Teams to coordinate tasks and interact with colleagues. During an outage, their ability to work effectively is compromised, leading to project delays, productivity losses, and increased stress and frustration. Similarly, freelancers and entrepreneurs who use cloud services to manage their activities may be unable to access files, process orders, or communicate with clients.

Security and Privacy Issues

IT failures can also expose individuals to security and privacy risks. Service interruptions can sometimes provide opportunities for attackers to exploit vulnerabilities and compromise personal data. For example, during the WannaCry ransomware attack, many individuals saw their personal files encrypted, with a ransom demand to recover them. Losing access to sensitive data, such as financial information, personal documents, and private photos, can have devastating consequences on individuals' lives.

Increased Dependence on Technology

The omnipresence of technology in daily life means that IT failures highlight our increased dependence on these technologies. The inability to access digital services can make individuals more aware of this dependence and the associated vulnerability. This awareness can lead to feelings of helplessness and frustration, especially when no quick solution is available to restore services.

Emotional Stress and Psychological Impact

IT failures can also generate emotional stress and psychological impact on individuals. Uncertainty about the duration of the outage, the inability to complete important tasks, and disruption of daily routines can cause anxiety and stress for users. For some people, especially those who depend on technology for communication and daily management, these interruptions can lead to feelings of isolation and worry.

Erosion of Trust in Digital Services

Frequent or prolonged IT failures can erode users' trust in digital services. Individuals may become more skeptical about the reliability of online platforms and cloud services, prompting them to seek alternatives or adopt more cautious backup behaviors.

This loss of trust can also affect consumption habits and reduce the adoption of new technologies.

In conclusion, IT failures have profound and varied effects on individuals, disrupting their daily lives, professional activities, and interaction with digital services. The growing dependence on technology means that service interruptions can cause significant inconveniences and create emotional stress. Anticipating these impacts highlights the importance of enhancing the resilience of technological systems and implementing support measures for users in case of failure.

5.4 Government Responses

In response to the devastating effects of IT failures on public services, businesses, and individuals, governments have taken measures to strengthen the security and resilience of critical infrastructures. Government responses to these events vary but generally include implementing strict regulations, promoting international cooperation, supporting research and development, and enhancing incident response capabilities.

Regulations and Legislation

To prevent service interruptions caused by IT failures, many governments have adopted specific regulations and legislation concerning cybersecurity and the protection of critical infrastructures. For example, the European Union implemented the Network and Information Security (NIS) Directive in 2016, requiring member states to strengthen the security of their networks and information systems. This directive mandates that operators of essential services and digital service providers implement adequate security measures and report major incidents to the competent authorities. Companies must comply with strict cybersecurity standards to protect their infrastructures from attacks and failures.

Similarly, in the United States, the Cybersecurity and Infrastructure Security Agency Act of 2018 established the Cybersecurity and Infrastructure Security Agency (CISA), which works to enhance the security of critical infrastructures nationwide. Additionally, regulations such as the California Consumer Privacy Act (CCPA) impose stringent requirements for personal data protection, pushing companies to adopt stronger security practices to avoid data breaches.

International Cooperation

Governments recognize the importance of international cooperation to combat global cybersecurity threats. Cyberattacks and IT failures know no borders, and transnational collaboration is essential to respond effectively to these challenges. For instance, the Global Forum on Cyber Expertise brings together governments, businesses, and international organizations to share knowledge and best practices in cybersecurity. Bilateral and multilateral agreements also facilitate information sharing on threats and incident responses.

International cyber incident simulation exercises, such as the Cyber Storm initiative organized by the U.S. Department of Homeland Security, test and improve coordination between governments and the private sector in the event of a large-scale attack. These exercises aim to enhance the overall resilience of critical infrastructures and prepare stakeholders to respond quickly and coordinatedly in the event of a major outage.

Support for Research and Development

Governments also invest in research and development (R&D) to improve the security and resilience of IT systems. Public funds are allocated to R&D programs aimed at developing advanced security technologies, identifying new threats, and creating innovative solutions to protect critical infrastructures. For example, France's National Research Agency (ANR) supports cybersecurity research projects through the RA-Cybersecurity program, which aims to strengthen defense and protection capabilities of information systems.

Public-private partnerships are also encouraged to accelerate the development and adoption of cybersecurity technologies. By collaborating with tech companies, startups, and academic institutions, governments can leverage innovation to bolster the protection of critical infrastructures. These collaborations promote the dissemination of cutting-edge knowledge and technologies in the field of cybersecurity.

Enhancing Incident Response Capabilities

Governments establish specialized agencies and dedicated cybersecurity units to enhance their incident response capabilities. These agencies work on detecting and preventing cyber threats, coordinating responses to attacks, and recovering from IT failures. For instance, the United Kingdom's National Cyber Security Centre (NCSC), established in 2016, plays a crucial role in protecting critical infrastructures and coordinating responses to cybersecurity incidents.

Training and awareness initiatives are also implemented to enhance cybersecurity skills among critical infrastructure employees and government officials. Certification programs, training workshops, and awareness campaigns aim to improve preparedness and resilience against IT failures.

In conclusion, government responses to IT failures involve implementing strict regulations, promoting international cooperation, supporting research and development, and enhancing incident response capabilities. These measures aim to strengthen the security and resilience of critical infrastructures, protect public services and businesses, and minimize the impacts of service interruptions on individuals. Cooperation and coordination at national and international levels play a central role in combating cyber threats and IT failures.

5.5 Business Adaptation Strategies

Businesses must adopt robust strategies to prepare for inevitable IT failures and minimize their repercussions on operations. These strategies include implementing preventive measures, preparing for crisis management, and establishing recovery plans. By investing in resilience and learning from past incidents, businesses can improve their ability to handle service interruptions.

Implementing Preventive Measures

One of the first steps for businesses is to implement preventive security measures to reduce vulnerabilities and prevent potential failures. This includes regularly updating software and systems with the latest security patches. Companies must ensure rigorous patch management to prevent known vulnerabilities from being exploited by attackers. For example, the spread of the WannaCry attack demonstrated the importance of timely patch application to secure systems against critical vulnerabilities.

Implementing advanced firewalls and intrusion detection and prevention systems can also help identify and block attack attempts before they cause significant damage. Businesses should also consider network segmentation mechanisms to limit the spread of failures and attacks within their infrastructure.

Employee Training and Awareness

Another key strategy involves training and raising employee awareness of cybersecurity best practices. Many IT failures are caused by human errors, often related to a lack of knowledge or vigilance regarding security. Companies should regularly organize training sessions for their employees, covering topics such as recognizing phishing emails, the importance of multi-factor authentication, and protocols to follow in case of suspected intrusion.

Creating continuous awareness programs helps maintain a high level of vigilance among employees and reduces the risk of human errors. By developing a cybersecurity culture, businesses can strengthen the first line of defense against IT threats.

Crisis Management Planning

Businesses must also develop crisis management plans to be ready to respond quickly and effectively in the event of an IT failure. These plans should include clear guidelines on communication during the crisis, mobilizing response teams, and service restoration procedures. Creating dedicated incident response teams composed of experienced crisis management members can facilitate the coordination of recovery efforts.

Regular crisis simulation exercises, or tabletop exercises, allow these plans to be tested and weaknesses identified for improvement. For example, simulation scenarios can include system failures, ransomware attacks, or data breaches. By learning to manage these situations in a test environment, businesses can better prepare to respond in a coordinated and effective manner in the event of a real crisis.

Disaster Recovery Plans

Disaster recovery plans (DRP) are essential to ensure business continuity after a major IT failure. These plans should include strategies for regular and secure backups to protect critical business data. Backups should be stored offsite or in secure cloud storage environments to ensure their availability in case of primary system failure.

Implementing automated restoration solutions and regularly testing recovery processes can ensure that sensitive data can be restored quickly and effectively. Businesses should evaluate their disaster recovery systems to ensure they meet their specific needs and can minimize downtime and data loss.

Adopting Multi-Cloud Strategies

To protect against service failures from a single cloud provider, businesses can adopt multi-cloud strategies. By diversifying their digital assets across multiple cloud providers, they can reduce the risk of widespread interruption due to a specific service failure. For example, businesses can deploy their applications and services on AWS, Azure, and Google Cloud simultaneously to ensure increased redundancy and resilience.

Using this approach also offers flexibility and cost optimization benefits, as businesses can choose the best services and offers from each provider based on their specific needs.

Monitoring and Analysis

Finally, businesses must implement real-time monitoring and analysis systems to quickly detect anomalies and security events. Advanced monitoring solutions, integrated with artificial intelligence and machine learning, can help identify unusual behavior patterns and prevent failures before they occur.

Analyzing security logs and previous incidents also allows defenses to be improved and proactive approaches to be developed to mitigate risks. By leveraging data and analysis, businesses can continually refine their cybersecurity and failure management strategies.

In conclusion, businesses must adopt robust adaptation strategies to minimize the impacts of IT failures. By investing in prevention, training, crisis management, disaster recovery plans, multi-cloud strategies, and monitoring, they can strengthen their resilience and ensure continuity of operations in the face of inevitable technological service interruptions. Lessons learned from past incidents highlight the importance of preparation and vigilance in an ever-evolving digital environment.

CHAPTER 6:
PREVENTING
FUTURE FAILURES

Having understood the severe consequences of IT failures, it is time to turn to preventive measures. This chapter details strategies and best practices to understand risks, enhance system security, and implement business continuity plans. Prevention is key to minimizing risks and ensuring the resilience of critical infrastructures.

6.1 Understanding Risks and Vulnerabilities

To effectively prevent future failures, it is essential to start with a thorough understanding of the risks and vulnerabilities to which IT systems are exposed. This understanding helps identify potential weak points and implement adequate measures to mitigate them. A proactive and well-informed approach is crucial to strengthening infrastructure resilience and ensuring service continuity.

Risk Assessment

Risk assessment is a fundamental step in understanding vulnerabilities. It involves a detailed analysis of the organization's technological assets, their value, and the potential threats they face. Companies must inventory all their digital assets, including systems, applications, and data, and evaluate their importance to daily operations. This inventory helps prioritize resources to protect based on their criticality.

Risk assessment also includes identifying internal and external threats. Internal threats can include human errors, hardware failures, and incorrect configurations, while external threats encompass cyberattacks such as malware, ransomware, and DDoS attacks. Analyzing cyber threat trends and the history of past incidents can provide valuable insights for anticipating and preparing for future attacks.

Vulnerability Analysis

Vulnerability analysis involves identifying and evaluating specific weaknesses in IT systems that attackers could exploit. This includes searching for security flaws in hardware, software, and configurations. Companies should use vulnerability scanning tools to detect known flaws in their systems and applications. These scans should be conducted regularly to ensure that all new vulnerabilities are identified and promptly corrected.

Penetration testing, or pentests, is an additional method for assessing system security. These tests simulate real attacks to identify weaknesses and evaluate the effectiveness of existing security controls. Pentest results help prioritize corrective actions and improve the organization's overall security posture.

Dependency Mapping

Dependency mapping is another crucial step in understanding risks. Modern IT systems are often interconnected, and a failure in one subsystem can have cascading effects on other parts of the infrastructure. By mapping dependencies between different systems, applications, and services, companies can identify potential points of failure and develop strategies to mitigate impacts in case of a failure.

This mapping also highlights critical dependencies on third-party providers, such as cloud services and SaaS applications. Companies should evaluate the risks associated with these dependencies and ensure their partners have adequate security and continuity measures in place.

Impact Assessment

Assessing the potential impact of failures is essential to understand the consequences of identified vulnerabilities. Companies should analyze the financial, operational, and reputational impacts of service interruptions. This analysis includes quantifying potential revenue losses, recovery costs, and the impact on customer satisfaction and company reputation.

Impact assessment helps justify investments in preventive and resilience measures. It also allows prioritization of security initiatives based on their importance for business continuity and maintaining customer trust.

Risk Management Roadmap

Based on risk and vulnerability assessments, companies should develop a risk management roadmap. This roadmap outlines specific actions to mitigate identified vulnerabilities and strengthen security measures. It should include clear objectives, deadlines, and responsibilities for each security initiative.

The roadmap should be dynamic and adaptable to respond to new threats and changes in the technological landscape. Companies should regularly review and update their roadmap to ensure it remains aligned with security objectives and operational needs.

In conclusion, understanding risks and vulnerabilities is a crucial step in preventing future failures and ensuring the resilience of IT systems. Risk assessments, vulnerability analyses, dependency mapping, and impact assessments help identify weak points and develop adequate mitigation strategies. By developing a risk management roadmap, companies can strengthen the security of their infrastructures and effectively prepare for future service interruptions.

6.2 Strengthening System Security

Strengthening IT system security is crucial to preventing future failures and protecting critical infrastructures against various threats. Companies must adopt a holistic approach and continuously adjust their practices and technologies to ensure the protection of their digital assets. Here are some key strategies to enhance system security.

Implementing Firewalls and Intrusion Detection Systems

Firewalls are essential components of IT security infrastructures. They regulate incoming and outgoing traffic according to predefined security rules, preventing unauthorized access and protecting networks against external threats. In addition to traditional network firewalls, companies should consider integrating web application firewalls (WAF) to protect web applications against specific attacks like SQL injections and cross-site scripting (XSS).

Intrusion detection systems (IDS) and intrusion prevention systems (IPS) are also crucial. IDS monitor networks and systems for signs of malicious activity and alert security administrators when a potential threat is detected. IPS go further by automatically intervening to isolate, block, or eliminate detected threats. A combination of firewalls, IDS, and IPS can provide a robust protective layer against intrusions.

Using Multi-Factor Authentication (MFA)

Multi-factor authentication (MFA) is a security method that strengthens account protection by requiring multiple forms of verification before granting access. In addition to asking for a password, MFA may require a second form of identification, such as a code sent to a mobile device or a fingerprint. This practice significantly reduces the risk of unauthorized access, even if passwords are compromised.

Implementing MFA should be widespread across all critical systems and applications. It should be integrated into user login protocols as well as authentication processes for administrators and privileged accounts.

Securing System Configurations

Secure system configuration is indispensable for minimizing vulnerabilities. This includes disabling unnecessary services and ports, configuring security settings according to best practices, and implementing strict access management policies. Companies should adopt a least-privilege approach, granting users only the permissions necessary to perform their tasks.

Security configurations should be regularly reviewed and updated based on new vulnerabilities and security patches released by vendors. Companies can use compliance management tools to automate these checks and ensure their systems are securely configured at all times.

Applying Updates and Security Patches

Regularly updating software and systems with security patches released by vendors is essential to protect against known vulnerabilities. Companies should establish automated processes to apply these patches promptly. The deployment of updates should be preceded by testing phases to ensure they do not interfere with normal system operations.

In addition to software patches, firmware and operating system updates should also be performed regularly. Companies should follow vendor security bulletins and cybersecurity authority guidelines to stay informed of the latest vulnerabilities and available patches.

Data Encryption

Data encryption is crucial for protecting sensitive information against unauthorized access. Companies should use robust encryption techniques to secure data in transit and at rest. Encryption protocols such as TLS (Transport Layer Security) should be used to secure communications between systems and users.

Critical data should be stored in encrypted databases and storage systems. Encryption keys should be securely managed and stored to ensure they cannot be compromised. Companies should also implement disk encryption solutions to protect data on user devices and external storage devices.

Continuous Monitoring and Incident Response

Continuous monitoring of networks, systems, and applications is essential to detect and respond quickly to potential threats. Security information and event management (SIEM) solutions enable real-time collection and analysis of security logs to identify suspicious behavior and security incidents.

Companies should also establish detailed incident response plans, including procedures for detection, communication, investigation, and remediation of security incidents. Dedicated incident response teams should be trained and equipped to handle attacks and data breaches, minimizing the impacts of incidents.

In conclusion, strengthening system security involves a combination of preventive and reactive measures. By implementing strong security controls, using encryption techniques, securing configurations, regularly applying updates and patches, and ensuring continuous monitoring, companies can effectively protect their infrastructures against threats and minimize the risks of future failures. System security is an ongoing process that requires constant vigilance and adaptation to technological advancements.

6.3 Employee Training and Awareness

Employee training and awareness play a crucial role in preventing IT failures and protecting critical infrastructures. Since many failures and security incidents are caused by human errors or careless behavior, educating employees on cybersecurity best practices is a key component of any IT resilience strategy.

Continuous Training Programs

Companies must implement continuous cybersecurity training programs for all employees, regardless of their role or level of responsibility. These programs should cover a wide range of topics, including basic cybersecurity concepts and more advanced aspects based on the company's specific needs. Training sessions can include modules on recognizing common threats such as phishing, secure password management, and acceptable use policies for IT resources.

The frequency and regularity of these training sessions are critical to ensuring employees remain informed about the latest threats and new security techniques. Training can be delivered through online courses, in-person workshops, webinars, and hands-on simulations to vary formats and maintain participant engagement.

Cyber Threat Awareness Sessions

In addition to continuous training programs, companies should organize regular awareness sessions to inform employees about the latest cyber threats and recent incidents. These sessions can include presentations on newly discovered vulnerabilities, post-mortem analyses of security incidents, and discussions on best practices for protection against these threats.

For example, recent case studies such as ransomware attacks and security breaches in known systems can be used to illustrate potential risks and prevention measures. These sessions help maintain a high level of vigilance among employees and reinforce the organization's cybersecurity culture.

Phishing Simulations

Phishing campaigns are one of the most common methods cybercriminals use to penetrate a company's systems. To educate employees on identifying and avoiding phishing attempts, companies can organize phishing simulations. These simulations send fake emails mimicking real phishing attacks to employees to test their responsiveness and ability to detect such messages.

The results of phishing simulations can be used to identify employees or departments needing additional training. Companies can provide constructive feedback to participants to help them understand the telltale signs of phishing emails and encourage them to report any suspicious activity to their IT security team.

Encouraging Incident Reporting

Companies should foster a culture where employees feel comfortable reporting any suspicious activity or potential security incidents without fear of repercussions. Clear communication on incident reporting procedures should be established, and employees should know how and to whom to report such activities.

Offering incentives for proactive incident reporting can also motivate employees to be more vigilant. By promoting a culture of shared responsibility, companies can detect potential threats more quickly and reduce the likelihood of unnoticed security incidents.

Developing Security Protocols

Companies should develop and distribute clear and detailed security protocols for employees to follow in their daily activities. These protocols should include guidelines on password management, the use of multi-factor authentication (MFA), safe web browsing practices, and secure handling of sensitive data.

Security protocols should be constantly updated to reflect the latest threats and industry best practices. Employees should be informed of updates and changes to the protocols, and training sessions should be organized to ensure they understand and adopt these new guidelines.

Specific Training for Administrators and Strategic Employees

In addition to general training for all employees, companies should provide specialized training for system administrators and employees in strategic roles. These individuals often have access to critical information and elevated system privileges, making them prime targets for attackers.

Training for these groups should include advanced topics such as privileged access management, secure system configuration, incident response, and vulnerability assessment. By developing specialized skills in these employees, companies can strengthen their defense-in-depth strategy and improve their ability to respond quickly and effectively to threats.

In conclusion, employee training and awareness are fundamental elements for strengthening system security and preventing failures. By implementing continuous training programs, awareness sessions, phishing simulations, and encouraging a culture of incident reporting, companies can educate their employees on cybersecurity best practices and reduce the risk of human errors leading to IT failures. Investing in cybersecurity training helps create a resilient infrastructure capable of withstanding evolving threats.

6.4 Developing Continuity and Recovery Plans

Business continuity plans (BCP) and disaster recovery plans (DRP) are essential to ensure that companies can quickly and effectively overcome service interruptions caused by IT failures. These plans outline the procedures to follow to maintain essential operations, restore systems, and minimize negative impacts on the business. Here are the main steps and considerations for developing robust BCPs and DRPs.

Identifying Critical Processes

The first step in developing BCPs and DRPs is identifying critical business processes. This involves a detailed analysis of the company's operations to determine which systems, applications, and data are essential for business continuity. Companies must prioritize based on the potential impact of interruptions on revenue, reputation, regulatory compliance, and customer satisfaction.

This identification helps create a hierarchy of technological assets, facilitating resource planning necessary to ensure their availability in case of failure.

Assessing Continuity and Recovery Needs

Once critical processes are identified, companies must assess their continuity and recovery needs. This includes determining the recovery time objectives (RTO) and recovery point objectives (RPO) for each critical process and system. The RTO defines the maximum acceptable downtime for restoring a service after a failure, while the RPO determines the maximum amount of data that can be lost, expressed in time, without significantly affecting operations.

These objectives must be realistic and aligned with the organization's technical capabilities. They serve as the foundation for developing recovery strategies and backup procedures.

Backup and Restoration Strategies

Data backup strategies are a key component of BCPs and DRPs. Companies must implement regular, automated, and secure backup solutions to protect critical data. Backups should be stored in diverse locations, including off-site and cloud storage environments, to ensure their availability in case of primary system failure.

Data restoration procedures must be clearly defined and tested regularly to ensure they work correctly. Companies should outline detailed processes for restoring systems and applications, prioritizing critical assets according to the established RTOs and RPOs.

Disaster Recovery Plans

Disaster recovery plans detail specific actions to restore operations after a major failure. These plans should include scenarios of various natures, such as hardware failures, cyberattacks, natural disasters, and human errors. Each scenario should be accompanied by a set of clear procedures to assess the incident's impact, mobilize response teams, and coordinate service restoration.

DRPs should also define the roles and responsibilities of each member of the response team, including contact information for internal and external stakeholders such as cloud service providers, technology partners, and regulators. Effective communication during a crisis is crucial to ensure seamless coordination and minimize downtime.

Simulation Exercises and Regular Testing

To ensure the effectiveness of BCPs and DRPs, companies must conduct simulation exercises and regular tests. These exercises allow plans to be tested under realistic conditions, identifying gaps and making necessary adjustments. Tests include system failure simulations, failovers to recovery sites, and backup restorations.

Results from exercises and tests should be documented and analyzed to continually improve plans. Lessons learned should be

integrated into procedures and recovery strategies to strengthen the organization's resilience.

Establishing Recovery Sites

Establishing recovery sites is another essential component of DRPs. Recovery sites, whether physical or virtual, serve as alternate locations to host critical systems and applications in case of a primary site failure. These sites must be equipped with the necessary infrastructure to support business operations, including redundant hardware, secure network connections, and access to backup data.

Companies should evaluate different recovery site options, such as secondary data centers, public cloud services, and recovery-as-a-service (RaaS) solutions. The choice of recovery site depends on specific RTO and RPO requirements, as well as cost and performance considerations.

Documenting and Updating Plans

BCPs and DRPs must be carefully documented and regularly updated to reflect technological and organizational changes. Documentation should include detailed instructions for each step of continuity and recovery procedures, as well as workflow diagrams and emergency contact lists.

Plans should be reviewed at least once a year or more frequently if major changes occur in the company's systems, processes, or infrastructure. Updates should be communicated to all relevant stakeholders and integrated into employee training and awareness programs.

In conclusion, developing business continuity and disaster recovery plans is crucial to minimizing the impacts of IT failures on business operations. By identifying critical processes, assessing continuity and recovery needs, implementing backup and restoration strategies, and conducting regular simulation exercises, companies can strengthen their resilience and ensure service continuity even in the event of a major interruption. Continuous review and updating of plans ensure their relevance and effectiveness in the face of technological advancements and new threats.

6.5 Technological Innovation for Better Resilience

Technological innovation plays a crucial role in improving the resilience of IT infrastructures. Advances in cybersecurity, data management, and recovery technologies enable companies to strengthen their defenses against cyber threats and ensure service continuity in case of failure. Here are some key technological innovations that contribute to better resilience.

Artificial Intelligence and Machine Learning

Artificial intelligence (AI) and machine learning (ML) are revolutionizing how companies detect and respond to cyber threats. AI and ML-based tools can analyze vast amounts of data in real-time to identify abnormal behavior patterns and suspicious activities. These technologies enable proactive threat anticipation and trigger mitigation actions before they cause damage.

Intrusion detection systems and security information and event management (SIEM) solutions integrating AI and ML provide a more accurate and faster view of potential threats. These technologies also automate certain incident responses, reducing reaction times and minimizing attack impacts.

Redundant and Fault-Tolerant Networks

Redundant and fault-tolerant networks are essential for ensuring the resilience of IT infrastructures. Advanced networking technologies, such as software-defined networking (SDN), allow the creation of flexible and adaptive network architectures. SDNs enable dynamic traffic redirection in case of a network segment failure, maintaining service continuity.

Network architects can also use mesh and multi-path techniques to ensure data can be routed through alternative routes in case of failure. Resilient networks combine physical redundancy with load-balancing capabilities to improve overall availability and performance.

Cloud-Based Storage and Recovery

Cloud-based data storage and recovery solutions offer significant advantages in terms of resilience and flexibility. Cloud service providers offer automated backup and recovery options, allowing critical data to be protected with frequent and geo-redundant backup configurations. In case of failure, companies can quickly restore their data from backups stored in different geographical regions.

Cloud storage architectures, such as object-based storage systems like Amazon S3 and Azure Blob Storage, offer high scalability and durability. Companies can leverage these technologies to create resilient storage environments capable of withstanding failures and ensuring data integrity.

Blockchain for Transaction Security

Blockchain technology is increasingly used to enhance transaction security and resilience against fraud. Blockchains offer a distributed and immutable architecture that ensures data integrity and prevents unauthorized alterations. This technology is particularly beneficial for industries such as finance, logistics, and supply chain, where transparency and traceability are crucial.

By using private or permissioned blockchains, companies can secure their internal transactions and create tamper-proof records of operations. Blockchain resilience stems from its decentralized nature, making it difficult for attackers to target a single point of failure.

Recovery as a Service (RaaS)

Recovery as a Service (RaaS) solutions offer rapid and efficient recovery of critical systems after an incident. RaaS solutions automate failover processes to secure backup environments using cloud infrastructure to minimize recovery times. Companies can configure automated failover policies to ensure critical systems and applications remain available even in case of a major failure.

RaaS providers offer monitoring, testing, and regular update services to ensure recovery environments are always ready to be activated. This outsourced approach allows companies to focus on their core activities while benefiting from resilience and service continuity advantages.

Zero Trust Security

The Zero Trust security model is an approach that does not implicitly trust any user or device, even if they are within the company's network perimeter. This method requires continuous verification of each access attempt based on user identity and authorization level.

Technologies enhancing the Zero Trust model include multi-factor authentication (MFA), privileged access management (PAM), and micro-segmentation to isolate critical systems and applications. By adopting a Zero Trust architecture, companies can reduce the risk of lateral movement of attackers within the network and limit the impact of security breaches.

In conclusion, technological innovation is a key factor in improving the resilience of IT infrastructures. Advances in AI and ML, redundant networks, cloud-based storage and recovery, blockchain, RaaS, and the Zero Trust approach are tools and strategies that enable companies to strengthen their resilience against IT failures and attacks. By adopting and integrating these innovations, companies can protect their operations, ensure service continuity, and improve their ability to overcome technological challenges.

6.6 Collaboration and Information Sharing

Collaboration and information sharing play a crucial role in preventing IT failures and protecting critical infrastructures against cyber threats. By working together, companies, governments, and cybersecurity organizations can strengthen overall resilience by exchanging knowledge, best practices, and tools to defend against attacks. Here are the main aspects of collaboration and information sharing in the field of IT security.

Public-Private Partnerships

Public-private partnerships are essential for strengthening cybersecurity at the national and international levels. Governments and companies must collaborate to share threat information, develop common defense strategies, and coordinate incident responses. These partnerships leverage the resources and expertise of each sector to enhance the protection of critical infrastructures and essential services.

Information Sharing and Analysis Centers (ISACs) are examples of these partnerships. They provide a platform for sharing threat information between companies in the same industry and government agencies. ISACs enable rapid and secure communication of information regarding ongoing attacks, discovered vulnerabilities, and effective mitigation techniques.

International Cooperation

International cooperation is crucial to combating globally widespread cyber threats. Cyberattacks do not respect national borders, and effective response requires collaboration between countries and international organizations. Initiatives such as the Global Forum on Cyber Expertise and the OSCE Cybersecurity Working Group facilitate transnational cooperation.

Countries can also sign bilateral and multilateral agreements to share information on threats, defense techniques, and best practices. These agreements strengthen collaboration between intelligence services, regulatory authorities, and incident response teams from different countries.

Real-Time Threat Information Sharing

Real-time threat information sharing is essential for a rapid and effective response to cyberattacks. Automated information exchange platforms, such as SIEM systems and indicator of compromise (IOC) sharing platforms, enable organizations to quickly share information on emerging threats.

These platforms facilitate the collection and analysis of threat data, providing companies with actionable intelligence to strengthen their defenses. Real-time sharing also allows for rapid identification of trends and coordinated attack campaigns, improving collective response capability.

Cybersecurity Communities

Cybersecurity communities, such as forums, discussion groups, and conferences, play an important role in knowledge sharing and strengthening collaboration among security experts. Events like the Black Hat Conference, DEF CON, and forums organized by the International Information System Security Certification Consortium (ISC)² allow security professionals to meet, share research, and exchange innovative ideas.

By participating in these communities, companies can stay up-to-date on the latest cybersecurity trends, discovered vulnerabilities, and advanced defense techniques. These interactions also foster the development of strong professional networks, offering collaboration and mutual support opportunities.

Crisis Simulation Exercises

Crisis simulation exercises, also known as table-top exercises, are important collaboration initiatives for testing and improving incident response preparedness. These simulations involve realistic crisis scenarios where participants must coordinate their responses and implement their incident response plans. Exercises can include organizations from various sectors, as well as government and international partners.

For example, the Cyber Storm initiative, organized by the U.S. Department of Homeland Security (DHS), is the world's largest cybersecurity simulation. It brings together public and private entities to test their ability to respond to complex and coordinated cyberattacks. These exercises help participants identify gaps in their plans, improve communication, and strengthen their resilience against real attacks.

Collaborative Research Projects

Collaborative research projects between academic institutions, technology companies, and governments also contribute to developing advanced cybersecurity solutions. Publicly and privately funded research initiatives explore new concepts and technologies to address emerging cybersecurity challenges.

These projects combine the resources and knowledge of various stakeholders to create robust innovations. For example, EU-funded programs like Horizon 2020 support cybersecurity research projects involving industry partners, universities, and research centers to develop innovative solutions focused on protecting critical infrastructures.

In conclusion, collaboration and information sharing are essential for improving the resilience of IT infrastructures against cyber threats. Public-private partnerships, international cooperation, real-time threat information sharing, participation in cybersecurity communities, crisis simulation exercises, and collaborative research projects enable organizations to prepare effectively, strengthen security, and respond quickly and coordinatedly to incidents. The synergy resulting from these collaborations helps collectively strengthen cybersecurity and protect critical infrastructures in an increasingly interconnected environment.

CHAPTER 7: THE MICROSOFT-CROWDSTRIKE INCIDENT (JULY 2024)

To conclude our exploration of IT failures, we examine a recent and relevant incident: the July 2024 outage involving Microsoft and CrowdStrike. This event allows us to see how the principles of prevention and incident response, discussed in previous chapters, apply in a contemporary context.

7.1 Brief Description of the Incident

Origin of the Incident

On July 19, 2024, a faulty update to CrowdStrike's antivirus software caused a global outage affecting many Microsoft services. The update introduced corruption in the "csagent.sys" file, a key component of the security software. This failure led to major disruptions in systems protected by CrowdStrike, notably impacting Microsoft Office 365 services.

Start of the Outage

The first signs of the outage were reported early on July 19, when users began experiencing issues accessing various Microsoft applications. The initial cause was quickly identified as a defective CrowdStrike update, deployed shortly before the interruptions began. The corrupted update caused system crashes, leading to critical errors and blue screens (BSOD), preventing computers from booting properly.

Nature of the Problem

The "csagent.sys" file from CrowdStrike, essential for the proper functioning of the cybersecurity software, was corrupted by the update. This corruption caused conflicts with Windows operating systems, leading to crashes and critical errors. The nature of the problem lay in the incompatibility introduced by the defective update, affecting system stability and preventing users from accessing their usual services. Microsoft and CrowdStrike engineers had to collaborate closely to diagnose and isolate the source of the failure.

Temporary Solutions

To mitigate the effects of this outage, Microsoft advised users to start their computers in safe mode to manually remove the "csagent.sys" file. This temporary solution aimed to restore access to affected systems by bypassing the corrupted component. Simultaneously, CrowdStrike worked on deploying a fix to permanently resolve the issue. Joint efforts by Microsoft and

CrowdStrike gradually restored affected services and minimized disruptions for users and businesses.

Permanent Solutions

CrowdStrike eventually announced that they had identified and deployed a fix to resolve the major IT outage affecting their services. The outage, which disrupted many users, was caused by a technical issue identified by CrowdStrike's team. The cybersecurity company assured that their systems were now stabilized and fully operational, minimizing the risk of long-term repercussions for their clients.

7.2 Spread and Initial Impact

Affected Services

The global outage affected several critical Microsoft services, including Office 365, Azure, and associated cloud services. Users experienced difficulties accessing their emails, documents, and other productivity applications. Businesses and institutions relying on these services faced significant interruptions, disrupting their daily operations.

Impact on Users and Businesses

The impacts were particularly severe in the finance, transportation, and media sectors. Airports, such as those in Sydney, Berlin, and Madrid, reported major disruptions, leading to flight delays and cancellations. Airlines like Air France and Delta Airlines had to manage cascading IT issues. In the United States, the 911 emergency call system was temporarily inaccessible, while in Australia, several banks, including the Commonwealth Bank, encountered difficulties processing money transfers. Supermarkets like Woolworths were also affected, with self-checkout systems down, creating long lines and customer frustration.

In Europe, telecommunications services were impacted, with problems reported by operators like Orange and TV channels such as TF1, CNEWS, and RTL, where broadcasts were disrupted by technical issues. The situation was exacerbated by the need for system administrators to manually remove the defective "csagent.sys" file, a lengthy and complex process for businesses with extensive IT infrastructures. In France, although the Orly and Roissy airports were not directly affected, they experienced delays due to disruptions faced by airlines. The Paris Stock Exchange also saw a slight decline, as investors worried about the economic repercussions of the outage.

Economic Impact and Corporate Reaction

The economic repercussions were immediate, with CrowdStrike's stock dropping nearly 17% and a 2.5% decline for Microsoft before the opening of Wall Street. The crisis management by both companies was initially criticized for its slowness, although communication efforts and corrective measures were quickly put in place to stabilize the situation.

This incident highlighted the increased dependence of critical infrastructures on cybersecurity solutions and underscored the need for greater resilience in the face of system failures. Companies were forced to reevaluate their risk management and business continuity strategies to better prepare for future disruptions.

7.3 Consequences

Short-Term Impact

The incident immediately caused massive disruption to the daily operations of millions of users and businesses worldwide. Organizations dependent on Microsoft services faced prolonged service interruptions, impacting productivity and revenue. Flight delays and cancellations, banking issues, and television service interruptions generated widespread frustration among customers and end-users.

Corporate Response

Microsoft and CrowdStrike were forced to react quickly to limit the damage. Fixes were deployed to resolve the problem, and recommendations were issued for users to restart their systems in safe mode to remove the corrupted file. This situation highlighted the need for companies to have robust business continuity plans to handle such crises.

Impact on Reputation and Trust

CrowdStrike's reputation was severely damaged, with a significant drop in its stock value. Microsoft also faced a loss of trust from its users, although the company managed to mitigate some of the damage by responding quickly and communicating effectively about the measures taken to resolve the issue. This incident underscored the crucial importance of software update reliability and security.

Implications for Cybersecurity

The incident raised important questions about the management of security updates and the resilience of critical infrastructures. Companies were urged to review their risk management strategies and strengthen their verification protocols before deploying critical updates. It also highlighted the need for close collaboration between cybersecurity service providers and their clients to ensure a rapid and effective response to incidents.

Lessons Learned

This incident served as a stark reminder of the inherent vulnerabilities in modern technological infrastructures. Companies learned the importance of redundancy and incident preparedness. Users also became aware of the need to follow best practices in IT security to minimize risks associated with software updates.

In conclusion, the Microsoft-CrowdStrike incident of July 2024 had profound consequences for businesses and users, emphasizing the need for increased vigilance and ongoing preparation in the face of potential cybersecurity threats and failures.

CONCLUSION

I T failures, whether caused by human error, technical failures, or malicious attacks, have profound consequences for our modern society. They affect public services, businesses, and individuals, revealing the growing dependence on technological systems in all aspects of daily life. Through case studies such as the WannaCry attack, the AWS outage, and incidents affecting Google Cloud, Facebook, Microsoft Azure, and Cloudflare, we have seen how these failures can paralyze operations, compromise security, and lead to significant financial losses.

To address these challenges, it is vital to develop resilience strategies that include understanding risks and vulnerabilities, strengthening system security, employee training and awareness, and implementing business continuity and disaster recovery plans. Technological advances such as artificial intelligence, redundant networks, cloud solutions, and blockchain offer powerful tools to protect critical infrastructures and improve resilience.

Moreover, collaboration and information sharing are essential to strengthen cybersecurity on a global scale. Public-private partnerships, international cooperation, crisis simulation exercises, and collaborative research projects enable the development of common strategies and rapid and effective responses to emerging threats.

IT resilience can only be achieved through a combination of

proactive and reactive measures. By investing in prevention, preparing robust crisis management and recovery plans, and adopting technological innovations, companies and governments can ensure that critical systems remain operational even in the event of major disruptions. Cybersecurity is a constantly evolving field, and it is crucial to remain vigilant and continue adapting to new threats.

This book has illustrated the importance of preparing our connected world for current and future IT challenges. By strengthening the security and resilience of our systems, we can protect our society against the devastating consequences of IT failures and ensure the continuity of essential services on which we rely daily.